My Weird School
FAST FACTS
Sports

Also by Dan Gutman

My Weird School

My Weird School Daze

My Weirder School

My Weirdest School

The Baseball Card Adventure series

The Genius Files

Flashback Four #1: The Lincoln Project

Johnny Hangtime

Rappy the Raptor

My Weird School
FAST FACTS
Sports

Dan Gutman
Pictures by
Jim Paillot

HARPER
An Imprint of HarperCollinsPublishers

To Emma

Photograph credits: page 11: Transcendental Graphics/Getty Images; 31: Transcendental Graphics/Getty Images; 40 © Bettmann/Corbis; 47: New York Times Co./Getty Images; 47 © Corbis; 54 © Oliver Berg/dpa/Corbis; 58 © Bettmann/Corbis; 65 © Bettmann/Corbis; 70: Rocky Widner/Getty Images; 70: Brad Mangin/Getty Images; 71: Jerry Wachter/Getty Images; 73: Jim Gund/Getty Images; 76 © AP Photo/Paul Vathis; 79: Kevork Djansezian/Getty Images; 85 © Rebecca Cook/Reu/Corbis; 91 © Bettmann/Corbis; 101: Sports Studio Photos/Getty Images; 102: Courtesy of Indianapolis Motor Speedway; 104: Christian Petersen/Getty Images; 108: Clive Brunskill/Getty Images; 111 © Car Culture/Car Culture/Corbis; 115: Doug Pensinger/Getty Images; 119 © YUTAKA/AFLO/Nippon News/Corbis; 128: Courtesy of Missy Parkin; 141: Kazuhiro Nogi/Getty Images; 146: Ronald C. Modra/Sports Imagery/Getty Images; 152: ullstein bild/Getty Images; 156 © Bettmann/Corbis

The author gratefully acknowledges the editorial contributions of Laurie Calkhoven.

My Weird School Fast Facts: Sports
Text copyright © 2016 by Dan Gutman
Illustrations copyright © 2016 by Jim Paillot
All rights reserved. Printed in the United States of America. No part of this book may be used or reproduced in any manner whatsoever without written permission except in the case of brief quotations embodied in critical articles and reviews. For information address HarperCollins Children's Books, a division of HarperCollins Publishers, 195 Broadway, New York, NY 10007.
www.harpercollinschildrens.com

Library of Congress Cataloging-in-Publication Data
Names: Gutman, Dan.
Title: Sports / Dan Gutman ; illustrated by Jim Paillot.
Description: First Edition. | New York : HarperCollins, [2016] | Series: My Weird School Fast Facts
Identifiers: LCCN 2015046350| ISBN 9780062306180 (hardcover) | ISBN 9780062306173 (paperback)
Subjects: LCSH: Sports–Juvenile literature.
Classification: LCC GV705.4 .G86 2016 | DDC 796–dc23 LC record available at http://lccn.loc.gov/2015046350

23 22 BRR 11 10 9
❖
First Edition

Contents

The Beginning 1

Chapter 1: Baseball 7

Chapter 2: Football 33

Chapter 3: Soccer 50

Chapter 4: Basketball 64

Chapter 5: Hockey 80

Chapter 6: Golf 88

Chapter 7: Automobile Racing 96

Chapter 8: The Need for Speed 103

Chapter 9: Other Sports 122

Chapter 10: The Olympics 137

Chapter 11: More Weird Sports Facts . . . 160

The Ending 166

The Beginning

 My name is Professor A.J. and I love sports.

Ewww, I said it! I said the *L* word! Ugh, disgusting. I think I have to go take a shower.

But the truth is that sports are the only things in the history of the world that I truly love. How come? In sports like football and hockey, you get to knock guys on their butts. In baseball you get to slide into home plate and knock the catcher on his butt. In basketball you get to dribble the ball down the court, charge in for a lay-up, and knock the defender on his butt. Knocking guys on their butts is fun.

Well, not as much fun as eating candy, but still fun.

The other cool thing about sports is counting how many times the players spit. Those guys spit *all* the time! I like to watch games on TV and keep track to see which team spits the most. That's just as much fun as keeping the *real* score.

Now just wait one gosh-darned minute there, Arlo!

 Oh no! It's Andrea Young, this annoying girl in my class with curly brown hair. She calls me by my real name because she knows I don't like it.

Yes, my name is Andrea, and I love sports, too. But knocking people down is mean, and dangerous. And spitting in public is disgusting.

I'll tell you what *I* love about sports. It's the mystery of not knowing how a game is going to end. When you go to the movies, you can usually tell in the first five minutes exactly how the story is going to end. The good guy's going to win. The bad guy's going to lose. The man and the lady are going to fall in love. It's so *predictable*. But in sports you *never* know for sure who's going to win until the game is over. That's what I love about sports. It's a big mystery.

Just ignore her. Andrea thinks she is *so* smart. She knows nothing about sports. Why can't a truck full of bowling balls fall on her head?

I, Professor A.J., will tell you everything you need to know about sports. For instance, did you know that the first sports were played by cavemen?

It's true! You see, back in caveman days a million hundred years ago, there was this guy named Ug. He came out of his cave one day with a club in his hand. He was going to go kill a dinosaur so he could have something to eat for dinner. But the next thing that happened was that some other caveman threw a rock at him for no reason. What a jerk, right?

So anyway, Ug took his club, swung it at the rock, and whacked it over the fence even though they didn't have fences in those days.

And that's how baseball was invented.

You made all that stuff up, didn't you, Arlo?

 Well, yeah. But I do know a lot of true stuff about sports, too. True, *weird* stuff. So if you want to know all that true, weird stuff, there's just one thing you have to do. Turn the page!

Hey, we're not going to do *everything* for you.

Yours truly,

Professor A.J.

(the professor of awesomeness)

 Andrea Young (I'm in the gifted and talented program.)

Chapter 1

Baseball

Some people have no luck at all. During a game in 1957, Richie Ashburn of the Phillies hit a foul ball that flew into the stands and hit a lady named Alice Roth in the head. It broke her nose.

That was bad enough. But then, as Alice was getting carried away in a stretcher,

Ashburn fouled off the next pitch. Guess where it went? Yeah, it sailed into the stands and hit Alice. It broke a bone in her knee!

That lady was *not* having a good day.

Deion Sanders is the only person in history to hit a home run in a Major League Baseball game *and* score a touchdown in the National Football League *in the same week*!

The most valuable baseball card in the world is a Honus Wagner card from 1909–10. In perfect condition, it's worth more than two *million* dollars.

If you ever find one of those cards,

there's one thing you should do with it right away—give it to *me*.

Why do they call it a "bullpen"?

A tobacco company named Bull Durham used to put billboards in the shape of a bull on the outfield walls of ballparks. Because relief pitchers took their warm-up tosses in the shade of those big Bull Durham signs, the pens they warmed up in came to be called "bullpens."

While many professional baseball players today make millions of dollars each year, the most money the legendary Babe Ruth ever earned in one season was eighty thousand dollars. If the Babe played today, he would probably make a million hundred dollars.

Of course, he would also be over a hundred years old. So forget about that idea.

 Do you know how Babe Ruth kept cool on really hot days?

He put a wet cabbage leaf under his cap. That's true! Every few innings he would put a new one in there. So be thankful that we have air-conditioning now. If we didn't, you might be walking around with vegetables on your head.

Babe Ruth at bat, c. 1923

 Gaylord Perry was a great pitcher, but he wasn't a very good hitter. One day San Francisco Giants manager Alvin Dark told some reporters, "They'll put a man on the moon before

Gaylord Perry hits a home run."

Then, in July 1969, just a few minutes after Neil Armstrong became the first man to step on the moon, Gaylord Perry hit his first career home run.

Why does a curveball curve?

Actually, *all* pitches curve. Even fastballs curve. They curve because the pitcher spins the ball as he throws it. When the ball spins, the flow of air around it is disrupted by the seams. One side of the ball spins in the same direction as the air rushing by it. The other side of the ball spins against the wind. This causes a difference in air resistance on either side of the ball, and the ball curves. See, you learned something here today.

 Cincinnati Reds player Johnny Bench could hold seven baseballs in one hand. That would come in handy when his wife asked him to take out the garbage, because Johnny could say, "I can't do that right now, honey, because I have my hands full."

 Why are left-handers called "southpaws"?

Back in the days when baseball was played mostly in the afternoon, ball fields were laid out so the setting sun would not

shine in the batter's eyes. For this reason, home plate was positioned to the west. Facing the plate, the pitcher's left hand was on the south side, so lefty pitchers came to be called "southpaws."

Or so the legend goes.

Do you know how the Atlanta Braves became the Atlanta Braves?

Well, they started out in Boston in 1871, and they were called the Boston Red Stockings. Then they became the Red Caps. In the 1880s, they were called the Beaneaters (that's right, because Boston is famous for baked beans). In 1912, they became the Boston Braves.

But they weren't done yet! From 1936 to 1941, they were the Boston Bees. Then they became the Braves again.

I guess they were exhausted from all those name changes, because in 1953 they moved to Milwaukee and became the Milwaukee Braves. And then, finally, in 1966, they moved to Atlanta and became the Atlanta Braves. Sheesh!

They should make up their minds!

Why is there a seventh-inning stretch?

According to legend, President William Howard Taft was attending a game one day. In the middle of the seventh inning, he suddenly got up from his seat. Thinking that the president was leaving the ballpark, everyone in the stands stood up to show their respect.

After stretching his arms and legs (he was over three hundred pounds), Taft sat back down and enjoyed the rest of the game. So did everybody else. And we've been doing the seventh-inning stretch ever since.

Speaking of sitting down, I think you should. Because this is going to blow your mind. Are you ready? Okay.

At least three Major League Baseball players (Moises Alou, Jorge Posada, and Kerry Wood) stated publicly that they *peed on their hands* to toughen them up or to prevent blisters and calluses.

Yes, you read that right. They peed on their hands!

Yuck! That's just gross. I think I'm gonna throw up. If you ask me, I'd rather have blisters than a handful of pee.

 Why does home plate have five sides?

Originally, home plate was a circle, like

a *plate*. In the 1870s, it was made into a diamond, like the field. But umpires had a hard time calling balls and strikes on the corners.

To correct that problem, those two sides were flattened in 1900 to create the home plate shape we know today. So home plate started out looking like a plate, and now, when you turn it upside down, it looks like . . . a little home.

In 1998, Sammy Sosa hit an amazing 66 home runs. He hit 63 the next season, and in 2001 he hit 64.

Incredible! And do you know how many times Sosa led the National League in homers during those three years?

NONE!

It's true. The first two years Mark McGwire topped him, and the last year Barry Bonds beat him.

But don't feel bad for Sammy. He led the league in homers in 2000 and 2002, hitting 50 and 49 those years.

The song "Take Me Out to the Ballgame" was written by Jack Norworth in 1908 after he saw a sign advertising a baseball game at the Polo Grounds in New York City. The amazing thing is, Norworth had never even been to a baseball game.

In fact, he didn't attend his first Major League ballgame until over thirty years later!

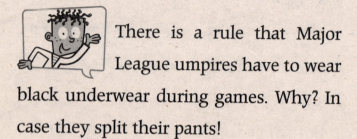 There is a rule that Major League umpires have to wear black underwear during games. Why? In case they split their pants!

If you ask me, it would be a lot easier if they just wore white pants.

Why is the pitching rubber 60'6" from home plate?

It used to be closer. But in the 1890s, a pitcher named Amos Rusie threw so hard that it was decided to move pitchers back so hitters would stand a chance against him.

According to legend, the distance was supposed to be increased from 55.5 feet to 60 feet. But a surveyor's poor penmanship resulted in the 60'6" distance, and they kept it that way.

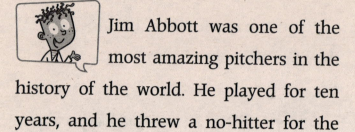 Jim Abbott was one of the most amazing pitchers in the history of the world. He played for ten years, and he threw a no-hitter for the Yankees in 1993.

But that's not the amazing part. The amazing part was that Abbott was born without a right hand! For *real*!

Luckily, you only need one hand to throw a baseball. And Jim Abbott was left-handed.

Hoyt Wilhelm, the Hall of Fame pitcher, hit a home run in his first Major League at bat in 1952. He played for another twenty-one years, and he never hit another home run.

In fact, over a hundred players have hit homers in their first at bats. And twenty-nine of them did it on the first pitch they ever saw.

Every year, over twenty-one *million* hot dogs are sold at baseball games. If you took all those hot dogs and lined them up end to end, people would think you were totally crazy. I mean, who goes around lining up hot dogs?

Why does every ballpark have a different outfield dimension?

The first Major League ballparks were built in the middle of large cities. To fit the fields and all the seats in, the parks had to be built between existing city streets. They couldn't move the streets, so they made the outfield dimensions different depending on the shape of the neighborhood.

What was the *worst* professional baseball team in the history of the world?

It had to be the 1899 Cleveland Spiders. They won just 20 games and lost 134. Ouch! Those guys were pathetic.

It should come as no surprise that the next season, there *were* no Cleveland Spiders.

* * *

Dave Winfield of the Yankees once killed a seagull while he was warming up during a 1983 game in Toronto! One of Winfield's throws hit the bird in the air and it died on the spot. I guess it was a "fowl ball."

Get it? Fowl? Foul? Ha-ha. That's a joke.

Anyway, it wasn't so funny to Winfield, because after the game he was taken to a police station and charged with cruelty to animals.

The next day the charges were dropped.

Why is the spitball illegal?

There are a few reasons the "spitter" was banned in 1920. Some people believed it was too hard to control, so it was dangerous to hitters. Others believed it hurt the pitcher's throwing arm. Still others believed that banning the pitch would add more hitting to the game. But most of all, the spitball was banned simply because many people thought it was disgusting and unsanitary.

As a side note, just two years before, 50 to 100 million people died from a flu pandemic. It was one of the worst natural disasters in human history. So people were really worried about catching diseases.

The biggest baseball bat in the world is at the Louisville Slugger Museum in Louisville, Kentucky.

Well, it's *outside* the museum. I don't think they could fit it inside, because the bat is 120 feet long and 68,000 pounds.

Something tells me that bat will never be used in a game.

 Did you hear about the seventeen-year-old girl who struck out Babe Ruth?

It happened in 1931. The Chattanooga Lookouts, a minor league team, was playing an exhibition game against the Yankees. Jackie Mitchell, a lefty sensation, was brought in to pitch to Ruth. After ball one, the Babe swung at and missed her next two pitches. The umpire called the next pitch a strike, and Ruth was out.

To make things even more amazing, Jackie struck out the next batter on three straight swinging strikes.

His name was Lou Gehrig.

On May 26, 1993, a baseball hit by Cleveland's Carlos Martinez bounced off outfielder Jose Canseco's *head* and went over the fence for a home run.

Canseco must have thought he was playing soccer.

You should have been there! Since you

weren't, search for it on YouTube. It's hilarious.

 Who invented the game of baseball?

Just about any dumbhead knows the answer is Abner Doubleday. Well, all those dumbheads are *wrong*. It's a myth. That means it's not true.

Doubleday was a Union general during the Civil War who fought in the Battle of Gettysburg. He even ordered the first shot defending Fort Sumter in the battle that started the war. But he wrote several books and many letters, and none of them ever mentioned baseball. There is *no* record of Doubleday inventing baseball or even playing the game in his entire lifetime. He never claimed to have invented baseball either.

There *is* one mention of sports in Doubleday's 1893 obituary. It said he was a man "who did not care for outdoor sports."

The shortest player in Major League history was Eddie Gaedel, who was three feet, seven inches tall. His career was also very short. Eddie came to bat one time as a publicity stunt for the St. Louis Browns on August 19, 1951.

It was the bottom of the first inning.

Eddie came out of the dugout swinging a bat. The number on his uniform was $1/8$. The pitcher, Bob Cain, laughed. Then he walked Eddie on four straight pitches (Eddie's strike zone was really small, you see). Eddie was immediately replaced by a pinch runner and jogged off the field to a standing ovation. That was the end of his playing career.

When Eddie died in 1961, the only MLB figure to attend his funeral was Bob Cain.

Why do umpires use hand signals for safe, out, and strike?

Back in the 1890s, there was a deaf-mute player named William Ellsworth Hoy. Because he couldn't hear the ump, Hoy had difficulty keeping track of the count. To solve the problem, he and his teammates asked the umps to come up with signals so Hoy could follow the game better. It turned out the signals helped everybody follow the game better, so they became a part of baseball.

Chapter 2
Football

Footballs are called "pigskins." Nobody knows why, because footballs are actually made out of *cow* skin. Do you think the pigs are jealous of the cows?

If I was a pig and somebody told me that footballs were made from cows, I would be relieved. On the other hand, I probably wouldn't react at all, because I would be a PIG! As far as I know, pigs and cows don't understand English.

By the way, do you know how many cows it takes to make a season's worth of NFL footballs? Six hundred! That's a lot of cows. If you took six hundred cows and you put them on a football field at the same time, well, it would really stink up the place, and nobody would want to play football there. That's a fact!

Somebody figured out that a cow has a 1-in-17,420,000 chance of being made into a football that gets used in the Super Bowl. Man, the guy who figured that out has too much time on his hands!

Something tells me that cows don't want to win *that* lottery.

Do you know why football players go into a huddle before each play?

No, it's not to keep warm. It was started back in 1892 with a quarterback for Gallaudet University named Paul Hubbard. Hubbard was legally deaf, so he gathered the rest of the team around him so he could hear them without the other team listening in.

The average NFL game takes around three hours to play. Do you know how

much of that time the ball is actually in play? Eleven minutes! The rest of the time the players stand around huddling, spitting, and scratching themselves.

As of the 2013 season, the average salary paid to an NFL player is about two million dollars a year. Two *million*! Do you know how much NFL cheerleaders get paid? Seventy to ninety dollars per game. That is totally not fair!

 What does guacamole have to do with football?

A lot. Because eight million pounds of the stuff get eaten on Super Bowl Sunday.

Not only that, but we also eat four million pounds of pretzels and eleven million pounds of chips.

And that's just in my uncle Milton's house.

Do you know why the Baltimore Ravens are called the "Ravens"?

Edgar Allan Poe lived in Baltimore, and he wrote a famous poem called "The Raven." Not only that, but the team's mascots are named Edgar, Allan, and Poe.

The biggest players on the field are nose tackles. Why would anybody want to tackle a nose?

But anyway, those guys weigh about 322 pounds.

Wow! Do you know who was the *smallest* player in NFL history? His name was Jack "Soapy" Shapiro, and he played for the Staten Island Stapeltons (the "Stapes") in 1929. Soapy was just five feet, one inch tall, and he weighed only 119 pounds.

What a shrimp!

In 1970, Tom Dempsey of the New Orleans Saints kicked an amazing sixty-three-yard field goal. But the length was not the amazing part. The

amazing part was that Dempsey was born with just half a foot!

That's not a joke. Go ahead and look it up if you don't believe me.

You know how everybody runs to the bathroom as soon as halftime comes? Well, during halftime at the Super Bowl, ninety *million* toilets get flushed in homes across America. Gross!

Of course, it would be a lot grosser if ninety million toilets *didn't* get flushed.

The Nerf football was invented in 1972 by Fred Cox, who was a kicker for the Minnesota Vikings.

College football players didn't have to wear helmets until 1939, and NFL players didn't have to wear them until 1943. Before that, football players wore fuzzy bunny ears on their heads.

Okay, I totally just made up that second part.

The waiting list to buy season tickets for the Green Bay Packers has eighty-six thousand names on it. So if you put your name on that list today, you'd have to wait almost a thousand years to get your tickets and see a game.

About seventeen million people watch each NFL football game

on TV. Do you know how many people watched the first televised game in their homes in 1939?

Five hundred! There weren't nearly as many toilets flushing at halftime in those days.

During World War II, a lot of professional football players served in the military, so there was a shortage of players. In 1943, the Pittsburgh Steelers and the Philadelphia Eagles combined to form the Steagles. In 1944, Pittsburgh teamed up with the Chicago Cardinals, and they were known as Card-Pitt. But when Card-Pitt didn't win a single game in the regular season, journalists instead called them the Car-Pitts, or "Carpets."

In 1997, Minnesota Vikings quarterback Brad Johnson threw a touchdown pass... to *himself*!

That's right. Johnson's pass was deflected up in the air. He caught it and ran it three yards for a touchdown. It was the only time that ever happened in NFL history.

Most NFL football fields in outdoor stadiums face north-south, rather than east-west. Why? Think about it. The sun rises in the east and sets in the west. If the field faced east-west, the team facing the west would get blinded at sunset.

 Are you ready for this? Before each game, Hall of Famer Darrell Green of the Washington Redskins would stuff Tootsie Rolls into his socks. Why? Nobody knows. Green said they made him run faster. Man, what a waste of perfectly good Tootsie Rolls. Personally, I would have used Kit Kats.

The Tootsie Rolls must have worked. Green won the NFL's Fastest Man Competition four times.

By the way, Marshawn Lynch of the Seattle Seahawks claimed that he used Skittles to turn him into "Beast Mode."

Football players are weird.

 You can't watch a full-length video of the first Super Bowl. Why not? Because the only videotapes they had from that game were erased. According to legend, a soap opera was recorded over Super Bowl I.

Guess which member of the Supreme Court also played in the NFL?

No, it wasn't Ruth Bader Ginsburg. It was Byron "Whizzer" White, who was a halfback for the Pittsburgh Pirates (now the Steelers) in 1938 and for the Detroit Lions from 1940 to 1941 and served on the court from 1962 to 1993.

President Teddy Roosevelt played a role in football history. The game was really dangerous in those days, and eighteen men died playing football in 1905 alone. Roosevelt was a big fan, and he held a meeting with college football officials to come up with ways to make the game safer. They changed the rules to make throwing the ball legal. So it's fair to say that football would not have passing if it wasn't for Teddy Roosevelt.

The first forward pass was thrown in 1906 by Bradley Robinson of Saint Louis University.

It was dropped.

The Dallas Cowboys haven't played in Dallas in more than forty years. AT&T Stadium, where the team plays, is in Arlington, Texas. So nah-nah-nah boo-boo on Dallas.

Was William Shakespeare a football fan?

The first time football was mentioned in print was in Shakespeare's 1608 play *King Lear*: "Nor trapped neither, you base football player."

I love Shakespeare. But I think he was talking about soccer.

Chapter 3
Soccer

Look, Ma, no hands!

According to legend, soccer was invented in London's Newgate Prison in the early 1800s. Back in those days people who were caught stealing things were punished by having their hands cut off. Ouch! So the prisoners started playing a game that didn't require hands.

Another legend has it that soccer developed when Greek and Roman villages would kick a human skull (yes, you read that right) to a nearby village square. That village would then try to kick the skull back to the first village.

Nowadays, of course, we're much more civilized. People *drive* from village to village, running over pedestrians along the way.

Everybody plays soccer! The Mayans played a game called Pok-A-Tok, where you could only touch the ball with your elbows, hips, and knees. The Romans played Harpastum. The Chinese played Tsu Chu. The Japanese played Kemari.

And the Greeks played Episkyros, a game that was played with no clothes on. Ewww, disgusting!

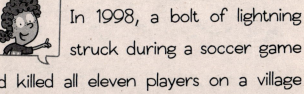

In 1998, a bolt of lightning struck during a soccer game and killed all eleven players on a village team in the Democratic Republic of Congo. That was sad. Nobody on the opposing team was harmed.

It's not unusual for a soccer player to run six miles during a single game and hardly ever touch the ball. And in baseball, it's not unusual for an outfielder to stand in one place for an entire game and *never* touch the ball. And it's not unusual for a sports fan to sit on a couch without moving for the whole day except to reach for the chips.

In 1994, all eleven players on the Bulgarian World Cup soccer team had last names that ended with the letters *OV*.

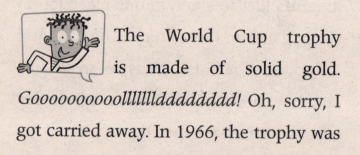

The World Cup trophy is made of solid gold. *Gooooooooooolllllllddddddd!* Oh, sorry, I got carried away. In 1966, the trophy was stolen from a glass cabinet just before the World Cup began in Westminster, England. A week later, it was found by a dog that was out taking a walk with his owner. The dog's name was Pickles.

That's not important, but I think it's cool to name a dog Pickles.

In 1983, the trophy was stolen again, and this time it was never recovered. I guess Pickles wasn't around to sniff it out.

 Did you ever count the number of panels on a soccer ball? Don't bother. There are thirty-two. That's one panel for each country in Europe.

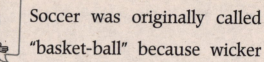 Soccer was originally called "basket-ball" because wicker baskets were used for the goals. And basketball was originally called "soccer" because it was usually played by people wearing socks.

Okay, I just made that second part up. But it's true that only in the United States and a few other countries is soccer called soccer. Most of the world calls it football. And in some countries it's called "Calcio" or "Nogomet."

Are you confused yet?

 I think it would be fun to be the queen of England, but not

all the time. Queen Elizabeth II loved soccer, but she wasn't allowed to play because she might get hurt. In her teenage years, she would disguise herself and join pickup games near Buckingham Palace.

 Do you know who Edson Arantes do Nascimento is?

That's the real name of Pelé, the most famous soccer player ever. I think he chose Pelé as his nickname because when people asked for his autograph, it was a lot easier to write Pelé than Edson Arantes do Nascimento.

But really, he chose Pelé because it means "six feet" in Brazilian Portuguese.

Pelé in the lead, 1975

Pelé was born with six toes on each foot. You heard that right, kids. Six toes. So he was one toe better than everybody else.

I wonder how good he would have been if he had *ten* toes on each foot.

 India refused to participate in the 1950 World Cup. Do you know why? Because their team was not allowed to play barefoot.

But at least they had no problem getting through airport security.

 In many of the poorer countries of the world, kids don't have soccer balls. So they play soccer using balls made out of rolled-up disposable diapers. No wonder soccer players don't want to use their hands.

 Until 1991, soccer was illegal in the state of Mississippi.

 Before 1862, when H. J. Lindon developed one of the first rubber bladders, soccer balls were made from inflated pig bladders. Ugh, disgusting.

Today, Pakistan is recognized as the "World's Greatest Manufacturer of Soccer Balls" and is the preferred manufacturer of game balls for all major FIFA tournaments.

Do you know what a bicycle kick is?

No, it's *not* when you kick a bicycle, dumbhead. A bicycle kick is when a player throws himself in the air and kicks the ball backward over his head. It's way cool. It's also a great way to land on your head and crack your skull open.

The most amazing thing in the history of the world happened in a semifinal match in the 1938

World Cup. Italian striker Giuseppe Meazza made a penalty shot. Well, that's not the amazing part, because players make penalty shots all the time. The amazing part was that just as he was about to take his shot, the elastic holding up his shorts snapped! Meazza held up his shorts long enough to score, and then they fell down!

Fortunately for Giuseppe, soccer games were not broadcast on TV in 1938.

 Can you juggle a soccer ball using just your feet, legs, and head?

It's really hard to do. But not for Martinho Eduardo Orige of Brazil. In 2003, he set the world record by juggling a soccer ball for nineteen hours and thirty minutes without stopping.

 What's even more impressive is that he did it without going to the bathroom.

Chapter 4

Basketball

Basketball was invented when some guy nailed two peach baskets up on the walls at both ends of a gym and told some other guys to see if they could throw soccer balls into them.

You probably think that's one of my jokes, but it's *not*! It really happened!

The guy was James Naismith. He was

a gym teacher at the school now known as Springfield College in Massachusetts. In 1891, he was asked to come up with a sport that would keep the athletes in shape over the winter when they couldn't train outside. Naismith dreamed up basketball, and the rest is sports history.

Of course, basketball back then didn't look much like basketball today. For starters, Naismith didn't have any basketballs! How could he? The game didn't exist yet. It's not like he could walk into a store and say, "I'd like to buy a basketball." They would think he was crazy!

"Get out of here!" the store manager would yell. "Security! There's a lunatic in the store who wants to buy basketballs!"

So when he first invented the game, Naismith used soccer balls.

Also, the backboard was made of wire. And dribbling was illegal. But the weirdest thing was that every time a player scored, somebody had to climb up on a ladder to get the ball out of the peach basket! Isn't that the most ridiculous thing you've ever heard? I wonder how long it took for somebody to come up with the idea of cutting a hole in the bottom of the basket.

 What Arlo didn't tell you (because he didn't know) is that James Naismith *also* helped invent the football helmet.

He was the center for his college football team, and he was getting beaten up pretty badly. His ears were swelling up from getting hit so much. One day, Naismith got kicked in the face so hard that he didn't recognize his teammates. While he was recovering, he and his girlfriend made a primitive helmet out of flannel. (*Flannel?* A lot of good *that* must have done!) Later, he made a better helmet out of leather.

 I knew that. But here's something that even Little Miss Know-It-All doesn't know: The tallest guy in NBA history was seven feet, seven inches tall! Do you have any idea of how high that is? It's even higher than my garage.

Actually, there were *two* players that tall: Manute Bol and Gheorghe Muresan. Bol was from the country of Sudan, and one time he killed a lion with a spear!

That didn't happen during a basketball game, by the way. That would have been scary.

One time I killed a spider in our bathroom, and I was freaking out.

Manute Bol

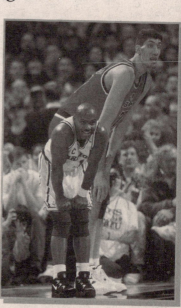

Gheorghe Muresan

Arlo knows a lot about basketball. But I'll bet he doesn't know this: the *shortest* player in NBA history was Tyrone "Muggsy" Bogues. He was just five feet, three inches. That's not much taller than I am!

The coolest thing was that during the 1987–88 season, Manute Bol and Muggsy Bogues both played for the same team, the Washington Bullets. So the tallest guy in NBA history and the shortest guy in NBA history were on the court at the same time. That must have been weird.

Can you spin a basketball on your finger?

It looks really cool, but it's hard to do. The world record for spinning a basketball on a finger with just one hand is ten minutes and thirty-three seconds. Wow! The guy who did it was a Spanish player named Ruben Alcaraz, who had too much time—and a basketball—on his hands.

Some people can even spin a basketball on their *elbow*! That's just weird. Tom Connors of England holds the record for the longest elbow spin: 6.14 seconds.

 Michael Jordan was probably the greatest basketball player ever, but after leading the Chicago Bulls to

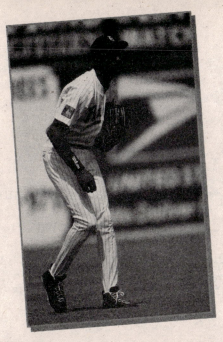

three NBA championships, he retired from basketball in 1994 so he could try something he always wanted to do: play baseball!

He played for the Birmingham Barons—a minor league baseball team. I guess he wasn't very good. His batting average was just .202. So after that Jordan went back to basketball and won three more championships with the

Bulls. It just goes to show that if you're good at something, you should stick with it!

 In 2008, something really amazing happened. Marc Gasol of the Los Angeles Lakers was traded to the Memphis Grizzlies. Well, that's not the amazing part. The amazing part is who he was traded for.

His own brother!

Pau Gasol was a Grizzly who was traded to the Lakers in the same deal. It was the only time in NBA history that two brothers were traded for each other.

And you know what's even rarer than that? Trading sisters. That has *never* happened in NBA history.

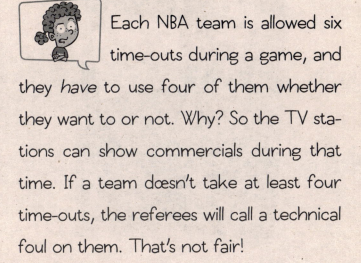
Each NBA team is allowed six time-outs during a game, and they *have* to use four of them whether they want to or not. Why? So the TV stations can show commercials during that time. If a team doesn't take at least four time-outs, the referees will call a technical foul on them. That's not fair!

How many games do you think it would take to score a hundred points?

Well, for Wilt Chamberlain, the answer is *one*.

On March 2, 1962, Wilt scored a hundred points in a single game for the Philadelphia Warriors. It had never happened

before that day, and it hasn't happened since that day.

Wilt was a really tall guy, so of course his nickname was Wilt the Stilt. Get it? Because stilts make you taller. I tried to walk with stilts once, but I kept falling down.

 A professional basketball court is ninety-four feet long. So how long do you think was the longest shot in basketball history?

If you guessed ninety-four feet, you're wrong! So nah-nah-nah boo-boo on you!

The longest shot ever made was 109 feet and 9 inches. Wow!

The guy who made that shot was Corey "Thunder" Law of the Harlem Globetrotters. He did it in 2013 in Phoenix, Arizona. Law and two of his teammates shot basketballs from that distance for an hour until Law made a basket.

Thunder (cool name, huh?) *also* holds the world record for the longest basketball shot backward over his head: 82 feet and 2 inches. That's just awesome.

Dunking is cool. When I get bigger, I'm going to dunk all the time. Even when I'm not playing basketball. Here are a few weird dunking facts. . . .

- In the 1986 NBA Slam Dunk Contest, Spud Webb beat Dominique Wilkins. The amazing thing is that Webb was five feet, seven inches tall, and Wilkins was six feet, eight inches tall.
- In the 2011 NBA Slam Dunk Contest, JaVale McGee dunked three balls in one shot! How is that possible? He jumped

up with two basketballs in his hands. After he dunked both of them, he got an alley-oop pass when he was still up in the air and dunked that ball too! Six points in one second!

- In 2010, a basketball team in Norway called Team Kangaroos slam-dunked twenty-eight shots in one minute. How did they do it? By jumping off a trampoline!

JaVale McGee at the 2011 Slam Dunk Contest

Chapter 5

Hockey

Back in the 1800s the first hockey pucks were reportedly made out of whatever the players could find, including—are you ready for this?—frozen cow poops!

Yuck! Gross! Are you kidding me? I guess that's why they play hockey with long sticks. I wouldn't touch one of those things with a ten-foot pole! No wonder goalies wear masks! Ugh! Was it just cold outside, or did they put the cow poops into a freezer? Either way, I think I'm gonna throw up.

The Stanley Cup has been awarded to the best team in the NHL ever since 1893. It was named after some Canadian guy named Lord Stanley. Guess which of these things have happened to the Stanley Cup over the years. . . .

    a. It was used as a cereal bowl.
    b. It was accidentally left by the side of the road.
    c. It was tossed into a swimming pool.

d. It was lost on a flight from New Jersey to Vancouver.
e. All of the above.

The correct answer is e.

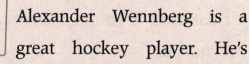 Alexander Wennberg is a great hockey player. He's known for his strong side-to-side movement. But the thing he's *best* known for is the time he scored a goal by dropping a puck out of his pants!

It happened in 2012. Wennberg was playing for a Swedish team called Djurgården. A bunch of players were fighting for the puck in front of the goal. Somehow, it became lodged inside Wennberg's pants.

He didn't know what to say. He didn't know what to do. He had to think fast! So Wennberg skated behind the goalie and squatted down until the puck plopped out of his pants. It was like he took a dump on the ice!

Goal! And it counted! You can't make this stuff up.

During playoff games in Detroit, fans will throw an octopus onto the ice in the middle of the game. Why? Because Detroit Red Wings fans are weird.

It all started back in 1952 when a pair of brothers named Pete and Jerry Cusimano threw an octopus onto the ice because an octopus has eight tentacles and that's how many wins the Red Wings would need to win the Stanley Cup. I don't know what one thing had to do with the other, but Detroit did win that year, so of course

Zamboni driver Al Sobotka with an octopus during a game between the Chicago Blackhawks and the Detroit Red Wings

other fans started throwing octopi onto the ice, too. That's how weird traditions begin.

During one game in 1995, the fans threw thirty-six of them onto the ice! I wouldn't want to be the Zamboni driver for *that* game.

Throwing an octopus onto the ice is weird. But that's not the only thing weird hockey fans have thrown onto the ice. . . .

- Cambridge, Massachusetts: a frozen chicken
- Florida: rubber rats
- Nashville, Tennessee: catfish
- San Jose, California: a shark!
- Toronto, Canada: waffles
- Edmonton, Canada: a slab of beef

This is probably the weirdest hockey story ever. Back in the 1930s, there was this Quebec goalie named Abie Goldberry. During one game, somebody shot a puck at the goal, and it bounced off Goldberry's jersey. But the weird thing is that Goldberry had a pack of matches in his pocket. The puck hit him, and the matches ignited. Then his uniform caught on fire! Luckily, his teammates were able to put it out.

Now *that's* weird.

 In the old Soviet Union, they used to train bears to play ice hockey as part of circus performances.

So now you know why there's no more Soviet Union.

Chapter 6

Golf

Golf is a weird sport. You know why? Because the person with the lowest score wins! In other sports, the person with the *most* runs, points, goals, or whatever is the winner. But with golf it's the opposite. That's why it's weird.

I don't know why anybody in their

right mind would want to chase a little white ball around a giant field all day. But my dad—and twenty-five million other people—do that every year. And that's just how many people play in America! They play that dumb sport all over the world, too. Nobody knows why.

So I'm going to let Andrea tell you her weird golf facts.

Why, thank you, Arlo! You're being so nice to me today! Are you feeling okay? Anyway . . .

Of all the sports in the world, golf is the only one that has been played on the *moon*.

It's true!

It happened in 1971, and the golfer was astronaut Alan Shepard. Shepard was the first American in space in 1961. Ten years later, he walked on the moon as part of Apollo 14. Disguising a portable six-iron with a sock, Shepard smuggled the club and a few golf balls on board the flight.

On February 6, while walking on the moon, Alan Shepard pulled out his golf club. The bulky space suit he was wearing made it so he could only swing one-handed.

Alan Shepard with his golf trophy

But gravity on the moon is one-sixth of the gravity on Earth. So when Shepard got ahold of one, it went "miles and miles and miles." So that was the longest golf shot in the history of the universe!

George F. Grant was an amazing man. He was a Boston dentist, the first African American professor at Harvard University, and also the inventor of the golf tee.

You know that little wooden thing that golfers put under the ball to raise it off the ground a few inches? Well, we didn't always have that thing. Somebody had to invent it. And George Grant was the guy who patented it, in 1899.

Before that, golfers would "tee up" the ball by building a little mound of wet dirt with their fingers. That was messy, and it was also a pain in the neck to get down on your hands and knees for each of the

eighteen holes on a golf course. So Dr. Grant, a serious golfer, devised a little wooden tee to do the job much more easily. It changed the game of golf.

Grant never made any effort to make money from his invention. He would hand out golf tees to his friends for free. Because of this, most people didn't know about his contribution to the game. It wasn't until 1991 that the United States Golf Association officially recognized Dr. George Grant as the inventor of the tee.

Do you know why golfers always have two pairs of pants?

Because they might get a hole in one.
Get it? Hole in one?

Okay, that's a joke. But speaking of holes in one, the most amazing thing happened on May 25, 1957. A guy in England named Edward Chapman got a hole in one on the eighth hole at a golf course in Richmond, Surrey. But that's not even the amazing part. The amazing part is that later that day, *another* guy named Edward Chapman got a hole in one on the sixth hole of that same course!

The youngest golfer to get a hole in one was a five-year-old boy named Coby Orr. It happened in 1975. Coby hit his tee shot right into the hole from 103 yards away on the fifth tee at the Riverside Golf Course, San Antonio, Texas. That kid was awesome.

Chapter 7

Automobile Racing

Hey, want to make a dollar? Tell your mom or dad you bet them a dollar that they don't know what "NASCAR" stands for. They probably won't. Tell them that NASCAR stands for the National Association for Stock Car Auto Racing. Then collect your dollar.

NASCAR champion Richard Petty's father, Lee Petty, was a race car driver, too. One time, he left a pit stop and did a full lap around the track with one of the guys in his pit crew hanging on to the hood of his car.

 The word "race car" is a palindrome. That means it can be read the same way forward and backward. My favorite palindrome is "Go hang a salami. I'm a lasagna hog."

A race car driver can lose five to ten pounds during a race just by sweating. Wow, I'm going to tell my mom that she should become a race car driver instead of going to Weight Watchers every week.

Why do they wave a checkered flag at the end of auto races?

Nobody knows.

But here's one theory: Back in the 1800s, there was a lot of horse racing in midwestern towns. When a race was over, everybody would go eat. So when they wanted to let everyone know the food was ready, somebody would take a tablecloth and wave it in the air. The tablecloths were usually checkered, so the checkered flag came to be known as the signal that the race was over.

 A car that's moving two hundred miles per hour will travel almost the length of a football field in one second. Wow, that's fast!

Come to think of it, a *turtle* that's moving two hundred miles per hour will travel almost the length of a football field in one second. But it's not very likely that a turtle will move two hundred miles per hour.

Unless it's driving a car.

And turtles don't drive cars.

But if they did...

The first Indianapolis 500 took place in 1911. The winner was Ray Harroun, and his average speed was less than seventy-five miles per hour.

Seventy-five miles an hour? My dad drives faster than that when we go visit my grandmother.

Oops. I'm not supposed to say that.

Do you know how many times the drivers turn right during the Indianapolis 500?

None! It was a trick question. They only turn left. And they do it eight hundred times during the race.

Hey, it would be cool if all the drivers turned around in the middle of the race and went in the opposite direction.

At the end of the Indianapolis 500, the winning driver always drinks a bottle of milk. It's true!

It all started in 1933, when Louis Meyer won his first Indianapolis 500. He pulled into the winner's circle and asked for a cold bottle of buttermilk to quench his thirst. Three years later, he won at Indy again and asked for a bottle of milk again. After that, it became a tradition, and all the winning drivers drink milk.

Wilbur Shaw drinking his victory milk, 1940

Chapter 8
The Need for Speed

 I like sports because sports move *fast*! Stuff that moves fast is cool. And sometimes stuff that moves fast crashes into other stuff. And crashing into stuff is cool, especially when it's moving fast.

Here's a list of some really fast stuff in sports....

23 Miles per Hour!

The fastest runner in the world? Believe it or not, his name is Bolt. Usain Bolt. Sometimes he's called Lightning Bolt. He's from Jamaica. Bolt has run a hundred meters in 9.58 seconds. That is *super*fast. If you don't think so, go out and run a hundred meters. It will take you a lot longer than 9.58 seconds. You might not get back until tomorrow.

So how fast can Usain Bolt run in miles per hour? About twenty-three miles per hour. That may not sound so fast compared to driving in a car. But remember, Bolt doesn't have an engine inside him! It's just his *legs* moving him that fast. I bet you can't even ride your *bike* twenty-three miles per hour on a flat surface. That guy is just awesome quick.

106 Miles per Hour!
That's about how fast the fastest baseball pitch was. It's hard to say for sure who threw it. There are a lot of pitchers who have thrown over a hundred miles per hour—Nolan Ryan, Aroldis Chapman, and Randy Johnson, to name just a few.

But of course, we'll never know for sure how fast pitchers threw before they had radar guns that clock the speed of a moving object. Old-timers like Bob Feller, Walter Johnson, and Satchel Paige may have been even faster than the fastest pitchers of today.

110 Miles per Hour!

The fastest hockey shot? According to *The Guinness Book of World Records*, it was made in 2011 at the Continental Hockey League's All-Star skills competition in St. Petersburg, Russia. Denis Kulyash from Russia, who played for a team called Avangard Omsk, hit a puck 110.3 miles per hour.

And hockey pucks are *hard*. I once ran into a tree chasing a Frisbee, and that hurt a lot. You don't want to get your face in the way of a 110-mile-an-hour slap shot.

163 Miles per Hour!

The fastest tennis serve? It was 163.4 miles per hour. How can anybody even *see* a ball hit that fast?

The person to hit that amazing serve was a twenty-four-year-old Australian named Samuel Groth. He did it at an ATP Challenger event in South Korea in May 2012.

Oh, by the way, having the fastest serve in the history of the world doesn't mean you're the best tennis player in the history of the world. When Groth hit

Samuel Gro

that 163.4 mile-per-hour serve, he was ranked number 340 in the world. And he lost the match that day to a guy named Uladzimir Ignatik. Try saying *that* three times fast.

235 Miles per Hour!

A lot of people think golf is a slow sport, but it can be *fast*. A golf ball coming off a tee goes from zero to a zillion miles an hour *in a hurry*! The fastest shot ever recorded was hit by Ryan Winther in 2014. Ryan hit a ball 235.1 miles per hour.

You can also play golf superfast if you put your mind to it. In 2011, a couple of Japanese golfers played 261 golf holes in

twelve hours. And in 2013, another Japanese guy successfully putted thirty-three balls in one minute on a practice putting green.

Those guys must have had to go to the bathroom or something. Why else would they be in such a rush to hit golf balls?

270 Miles per Hour!

The fastest car in the world? John Hennessey's Hennessey Venom GT. It was tested out on a runway that NASA used for space shuttle landings, and it got up to 270.49 miles per hour. That is *insane* fast! My dad is afraid to drive his car faster than seventy-five miles per hour.

I hope there weren't any cops around when that Hennessey Venom GT was going so fast. Because that car was definitely going to get a ticket.

My name is Andrea, and I like things *sssssslllllooooowwww*. Slow and steady wins the race. That's what I always say.

Did you ever hear the story of the tortoise and the hare? It's an Aesop's fable. There's this hare, which is like a rabbit. He was bragging about how fast he could run. The hare was really full of himself, sort of like Arlo.

Anyway, he was making fun of a nice tortoise, laughing about how slow the tortoise moved. Well, the tortoise challenged the hare to a race. Of course the hare accepted the challenge, and all the animals gathered for the big race.

The hare jumped out in front, naturally. He got so far ahead that he decided to lay down and take a nap. By the time he woke up, guess what had happened? Yes, the tortoise—moving slowly and steadily—caught up. The hare made a dash for the finish line, but it was too late. The tortoise had won.

Like I said, slow and steady wins the race.

 If you ask me, the most amazing part of Andrea's story is that the hare and the tortoise were able to talk to each other.

Oh hush, Arlo.

Anyway, that's why I like things *sssssslllllooooowwww*. For instance, did you know that some cricket games take *days* to finish? After all that, the game will sometimes end in a tie.

Bicycle racing is like that, too. The bikes can go pretty fast, but the races can go on forever. The most famous bike race of them all—the Tour de France—takes twenty-one days to finish. Twenty-one *days*! That's slow!

The Tour de France, 2013

Hey, Andrea! Did you know that the life span of a drone ant is about three weeks?

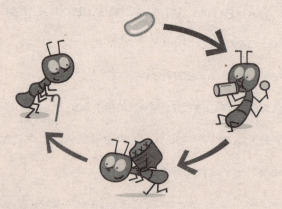

 What does that have to do with anything, Arlo?

 Well, that means a drone ant could be born, live its whole life, and die without ever knowing who won the Tour de France bicycle race!

I feel sorry for drone ants. They don't live very happy lives to begin with. And then you have to add on top of that the fact that they can't even watch a bicycle race. It's a tough life.

Ignore Arlo. He just wants attention.

Another slow game is bowling. Even the strongest bowlers only throw that big, heavy ball about twenty miles per hour.

Lacrosse looks like a really fast sport, but when it was first invented in Canada, they

had up to a thousand players on the field and a game took two or three days!

Speaking of slow games, how about chess? Sometimes it seems like the players aren't moving at *all* for hours at a time.

But then they have speed chess, where they play the game really fast and it's over in a few minutes. They even have different kinds of speed chess. Blitz chess is faster than Rapid chess, and Bullet chess is faster than Blitz chess. The players have to *think* fast.

Another slow sport is curling. Did you ever see curling during the Olympics? It's really cool. The players slide this heavy polished granite stone down a sheet of

ice and try to make it stop on a target while their teammates run in front sweeping the ice with a broom. Curling looks like a combination of shuffleboard and cleaning your house. It's really popular in Canada.

But there's one sport that's slower than *all* of them.

Snail racing.

Yes, snail racing is a thing! I didn't make it up. It's popular in England. In fact, every year, in the village of Congham, they hold the World Snail Racing Championship.

The owners of the snails put little racing numbers on the shells and then place the snails in the middle of a thirteen-inch circle. A snail trainer shouts, "Ready . . . steady . . . slow!" and the snails take off.

Well, sometimes they just sit there and don't do anything. But the snail that makes it to the edge of the circle first is the winner. A fast-moving snail might move thirteen inches in a little over two minutes.

Now *that's* slow!

Chapter 9

Other Sports

Skating

The first skate blades were made from the bones of horses, cows, and deer. That must have been weird to strap cow bones to your feet. But it would be a lot weirder if cows were strapping human bones to their feet and skating around on them.

The jump called the axel didn't get its name because the skater spins around an axle. It was named after Axel Paulsen, a speed skater and figure skater from Norway. He was the first to land the jump, in 1882.

Similarly, Swedish skater Ulrich Salchow invented the jump that came to be named after him, the salchow. And the lutz is

Axel Paulsen

Ulrich Salchow at the 1908 Summer Olympics

named after Alois Lutz from Austria.

Someday maybe I'll invent a new jump and it will be called the Andrea.

 Skaters will sometimes spin more than three hundred revolutions per minute, and their arms may be subjected to more than four Gs.

Wow, I'm surprised that skaters' eyeballs don't fall out of their sockets.

Skiing

 Someday you may ski on the moon. When American astronaut Harrison Schmitt walked on the moon in 1972, he said that the mountains in the Sea of Serenity would make a great location for "lunar skiing holidays."

There's a ski resort in Dubai where the average temperature is over ninety degrees.

What?!

How is that possible? Well, the ski resort is indoors. Ski Dubai has five slopes of man-made snow, a toboggan run, a body slide, and an ice cave.

It also has penguins, and after you finish skiing you can go hang out with them. I wish I could go run away to Dubai and live with the penguins.

Rugby

 Do you know why the sport of rugby is called rugby?

I'm not going to tell you.

Okay, okay, I'll tell you.

The game isn't played on a rug. And it has nothing to do with bees. Rugby is called rugby because it was started in 1823 at a British school called Rugby School!

I know; that was your next guess.

According to legend, the game began when a student named William Webb Ellis was playing soccer, and he suddenly picked the ball up in his hands and started running with it.

Bowling

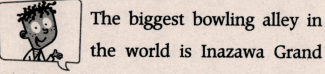

The biggest bowling alley in the world is Inazawa Grand Bowl in Inazawa City, Japan. It has 116 lanes! Wow! That's a lot of lanes! If you took 116 bowling lanes and you lined them up right next to each other . . . it would look pretty much like a bowling alley. Because that's what bowling alleys are—lanes lined up next to each other!

At Inazawa Grand Bowl, 696 people can bowl at the same time. I feel sorry for the guy who runs the shoe rental desk at that place.

Tennis

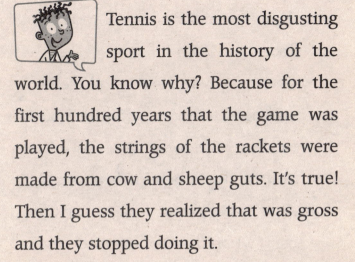

Tennis is the most disgusting sport in the history of the world. You know why? Because for the first hundred years that the game was played, the strings of the rackets were made from cow and sheep guts. It's true! Then I guess they realized that was gross and they stopped doing it.

Tennis balls used to be gross, too. Back in the old days, they were stuffed with human hair! Yuck!

There are lots of things people do with tennis balls besides play tennis. This is for real. . . .

- You can put them on the bottom of chair legs so they don't scrape the floor.
- You can cover them with Vaseline and hang them outside your house to keep bugs away.
- You can hang one inside your garage to help your parents park the car. (When the tennis ball touches the windshield, it's time to stop.)
- You can drill a hole in one to make a home for pet mice.
- You can put one on the end of a

broom to rub scuff marks off floors.
- You can toss a few into the dryer to help your clothes dry faster.
- You can cut one in half and use it to make it easier to open jars.
- You can stop snoring if you attach one to the back of your pajamas so you can't sleep on your back. (Most snorers only snore while sleeping on their backs.)

Evonne Goolagong was a tennis player from Australia who came from an Aboriginal family. Aborigines are the native people of Australia, and they have faced a lot of discrimination

there. But Goolagong became a tennis star and won fourteen Grand Slam titles.

That was pretty amazing. But what is even *more* amazing is that, in the Aboriginal language, the last name Goolagong means "kangaroo's nose."

Table Tennis

Thomas Edison invented the lightbulb. The Wright brothers

invented the first successful airplane. Alexander Graham Bell invented the telephone. And in 1880, a British engineer named James Gibb invented the Ping-Pong ball.

Hey, somebody had to.

Gibb actually gets credit for inventing the game of table tennis itself. He wanted to create a game he could play indoors when it was raining.

In those early days, table tennis was called Flim-Flam, Gossima, and Whiff Whaff. But in 1901, an equipment manufacturer renamed it Ping-Pong, and that's when the sport became a big success.

Table tennis was banned in the Soviet Union from 1930 to 1950. The powers that be thought it was bad for your eyes!

Volleyball

Volleyball and basketball were invented just nine miles from each other in Massachusetts and within four years of each other.

As you know, basketball was invented in Springfield by James Naismith in 1891. Volleyball was invented right up the road in Holyoke by William George Morgan in 1895. In fact, Naismith and Morgan were both gym teachers, and they even knew each other!

Morgan saw that basketball involved a lot of running, and it was difficult for some people to play. He wanted to create a game that *anybody* in his classes could play, so he combined some parts of tennis, badminton, and handball. The result: volleyball!

Of course, there are a lot of great athletes who play volleyball and a lot of terrible athletes who play basketball (like Arlo and his friends!).

At first, Morgan used basketballs. But he realized that basketballs were too heavy for volleyball. Next, he tried just using the rubber bladder that was inside a basketball. But that was too light. So he asked the Spalding company (started by baseball star Albert Spalding) to design a ball specifically for volleyball, and they made one that was just right.

It was sort of like the story of the three bears when you think about it.

Chapter 10

The Olympics

I hate to break it to you, but the gold medals they give out during the Olympics are *not* made of gold. And they haven't been made out of gold since 1912!

It's true. Gold medals are actually made of silver. And they're not even *completely* made of silver! A gold medal is 93 percent silver and 6 percent copper.

So let's see: 93 plus 6 equals 99. What about the other 1 percent?

Oh, that's the gold finish. That's what makes the medal look gold. So if you win a gold medal, you won a silver medal. And if you win a silver medal, you won a silver medal. And there isn't even anything you can dig out of the ground called bronze. Bronze is just a combination of copper and tin.

Do you know why the five rings on the Olympic flag are yellow, green, red, black, and blue?

Neither did I. But I looked it up in my encyclopedia. That's how you learn new things! Those colors were chosen in 1912 because at least one of them appeared in every flag in the world.

Oh, by the way, those five rings represent Africa, Asia, Australia, Europe, and the Americas. They're linked together on the Olympic flag to show that people all over the world can be joined together in respect for one another.

See? You learned something today. Isn't learning new stuff fun?

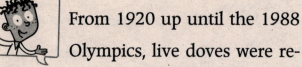 From 1920 up until the 1988 Olympics, live doves were released during opening ceremonies. Oh, it must have been a glorious sight—hundreds of beautiful white birds flying majestically across the sky to symbolize peace in the world.

Unfortunately, at the 1988 Olympics that summer in South Korea, some of the doves decided to fly over to the Olympic torch just as they were lighting it. I don't think I need to tell you what happened next. But they could have served roast dove at the Olympic snack bar that day.

 Before 1984, China had not won a single Olympic medal.

Just twenty-four years later, when China hosted the 2008 Olympics, they won a *hundred* medals. They also won more gold medals (fifty-one) than any other nation.

Benjamin Franklin was a great American and one of our Founding Fathers. He also discovered many things about electricity and invented the

Franklin stove. What most people *don't* know is that he also invented flippers, those things you put on your feet to help you swim faster.

This is what happened: Ben was out swimming one day, and it looked like a storm was coming. He didn't want to get struck by lightning, so he tried to swim really fast so he could get home and warm up in front of his Franklin stove.

Okay, I made that last part up. But Benjamin Franklin really *did* invent swim fins. And he did it when he was just eleven years old. This is what he wrote about it years later. . . .

When a youth, I made two oval pallets, each about ten inches long, and six broad, with a hole for the thumb, in order to retain it fast in the palm of my hand. They much resembled a painter's pallets. In swimming I pushed the edges of these forward, and I struck the water with their flat surfaces as I drew them back. I remember I swam faster by means of these pallets, but they fatigued my wrists. I also fitted to the soles of my feet a kind of sandals, but I was not satisfied with them, because I observed that the stroke is partly given by the inside of the feet and the ankles, and not entirely with the soles of the feet.

Swimmers will do anything to swim faster. And I mean *anything*. Competitive swimmers even shave off their body hair before a race because it allows them to swim just a little bit faster. Races are often decided by hundredths of a second, so the athletes will shave the hair off their arms, legs, back, and chest. Every little bit counts. Some swimmers even shave their hands and feet.

Shaving your feet? Now, *that's* weird.

 I don't care what you shave off. You can shave off your eyelashes. You can shave off your toenails for all I care. You're still not going to swim faster than a sailfish.

They are the fastest swimmers in the world. A sailfish can swim one hundred meters in less than five seconds. That's about ten times as fast as the fastest human being.

Not only can sailfish swim really fast, they can also change the color of their body to confuse predators. So a sailfish can be gray one minute, and as soon as some shark or something starts chasing it, the sailfish can turn blue and go hide behind an underwater bush or something and say, "You can't catch me, shark. Nah-nah-nah boo-boo!"

Sailfish are cool.

Weird Olympic Sports

You think synchronized swimming, biathlon, and curling are weird Olympic sports? Back in 1908, tug-of-war was an Olympic sport. Yes, teams would pull on each end of a rope trying to drag the other team past a line.

Think that's weird?

There used to be an Olympic sport called swimming obstacle course. In the 1900 Olympics, swimmers had to swim under boats, climb across a row of boats, and climb over a pole to reach the finish line.

Think *that's* weird?

The same year, live pigeon shooting was an Olympic sport. Almost three hundred birds were killed.

Think *that's* weird?

Rope climbing was an Olympic sport from 1896 until 1932. Yes, guys would race to climb up ropes.

Think *that's* weird?

Club swinging was an Olympic sport in 1904. The athlete would hold a club that looked like a bowling pin in each hand. Then he would swing them around. Points would be awarded for how well he did it and how complicated his movements were.

Think *that's* weird?

You're right, it was. That's why they got rid of all those dumb sports.

Henry Pearce of Australia was a real animal lover. During the 1928 Olympics in Amsterdam, he stopped rowing in the middle of his race so a family of ducks could pass in front of his boat. Even so, Pearce still won the gold medal. I think the ducks should have won.

At the Olympic Games in 1900, there were more athletes than spectators.

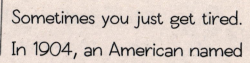 Sometimes you just get tired. In 1904, an American named Fred Lorz won the Olympic marathon. Or it seemed that way at first. Then it was discovered that he'd stopped running after nine miles and hopped into an official's car for the next eleven miles!

Unfortunately for Lorz, the car broke down, and the poor guy actually had to finish the race on foot. That would have been weird if he reached the finish line in a car!

Lorz was banned for life by the Amateur Athletic Union. But then he apologized and all was forgiven. The next year, he won the Boston Marathon fair and square.

The founder of the modern Olympic Games is a French guy named Baron Pierre de Coubertin. He must have really liked art. At the 1900 Olympics in Paris, the first-place winners didn't get medals. They were awarded (are you ready for this?) paintings!

But *this* fast fact is even *more* amazing. In 1912, an arts competition was added to the Olympic Games. That's right! They gave Olympic medals for *art*!

And guess who won the gold medal for literature?

It was Baron Pierre de Coubertin! He wrote a poem titled "Ode to Sport."

If you ask me, they should have given him the Nobel Prize. That's a prize they give out to people who don't play sports.

Before he became the world-famous boxer Muhammad Ali, he was just a scared eighteen-year-old named Cassius Clay. Clay hated flying, and when he found out that he would have to fly to Italy in order to box in the 1960 Olympics, Clay asked if he could take a boat there instead. His coach talked him into flying, but Clay was so nervous that he bought a parachute from an army surplus store and wore it during the entire flight to Rome.

 In just one day at the 1904 Olympics, American gymnast George Eyser won *six* medals, including three golds. That was amazing in itself. But that's not even the amazing part of the story.

The most amazing part was that Eyser only had one leg! His left one had to be amputated after it was run over by a train.

Johnny Weissmuller was one of the greatest swimmers in Olympic history. He won five gold medals at the 1924 and 1928 games. But that's not what made him famous. After his Olympic career was over, he went to Hollywood and became a movie star playing Tarzan, a boy who was raised by apes in the African jungle.

Weissmuller starred in a dozen Tarzan movies, including *Tarzan, the Ape Man; Tarzan's Secret Treasure; Tarzan's New York Adventure; Tarzan and the Leopard Woman;* and *Tarzan and the Mermaids.*

In the ancient Olympics in Greece, only men were allowed to participate, and *all* the athletes performed in the nude.

Ugh! Gross! Disgusting! I think I'm gonna throw up!

But it's true. In fact, the word "gymnasium" comes from the Greek word "gymnos," which means "naked."

I guess those guys saved a lot of money on sweatpants and T-shirts and underwear.

 Do you think *you* could win an Olympic medal?

A ten-year-old boy won a medal in the 1896 Olympics in Athens, Greece. His name was Dimitrios Loundras. He was a gymnast, competing in the team parallel bars event. Dimitrios won a bronze medal, making him the youngest person in the history of the world to win an Olympic medal.

He grew up to become an admiral in the Greek navy, and he was also the last living athlete from the 1896 Olympics. Dimitrios died in 1971.

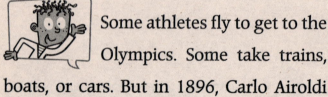
Some athletes fly to get to the Olympics. Some take trains, boats, or cars. But in 1896, Carlo Airoldi *walked* to the Olympics.

That's right. Airoldi was a marathon runner for Italy. So he walked from Milan to Greece, which is more than a *thousand* miles.

But then the weirdest thing in the history of the world happened. Somebody found out that Airoldi had accepted a prize for winning another race, so he was not an amateur, and not allowed to compete in the Olympics.

He walked a thousand miles only to find out that he had been disqualified. Bummer in the Summer Olympics!

Chapter 11

More Weird Sports Facts

My name is A.J. and I hate just two days of the year: the day before baseball's All-Star Game and the day after baseball's All-Star Game.

Do you know why I hate those two days? Because those are the only days all year long when there are no professional sports games going on in America!

None! No baseball. No basketball. No hockey. No football.

There's nothing to watch on TV!

Here's a sport that hasn't caught on in America yet: wife carrying.

I didn't make that up. YouTube it if you don't believe me. In Finland, there's really a sport where men run around a track while carrying their wives! Why do they do this? Nobody knows.

But the official course is 253.5 meters, and it's an obstacle course. So the husbands have to run, jump into a pool of water, run some more, climb over a log, and run some

more—and the whole time they have to carry their wives on their backs!

According to the International Wife Carrying Competition Rules Committee (yes, that's a thing), the men can carry their own wife or a neighbor's wife, but all wives must be over seventeen years old.

The world champion wife-carrying team from 2009 to 2013 was Taisto Miettinen and Kristiina Haapanen—of Finland, of course.

If you moved to Thailand, you could get a job as a professional kite flyer. Yes, kites are so popular that kite flying is a professional sport there. The people are nutty for kites!

Back in the thirteenth century, during wars they would send up kites with gunpowder and fuses in them and blow them up over enemy territory. That must have been cool.

In many sports, the home team wears white uniforms, while the visiting teams wear gray or a darker color. Why? Take a guess.

Well, you're wrong!

This custom started in the early days of professional baseball. Visiting teams that were on the road didn't have their own washing machines, of course. So it was hard for them to keep their uniforms clean. If they wore darker colors, they could hide the dirt and grass stains more easily. The home team could wash their uniforms anytime, so they wore white.

What's the most popular sport in the world?

That depends on who you ask and what you mean by "popular." If you ask a website called Sporteology and popular means "most watched," the answer is soccer.

After soccer, the top ten most popular sports are: cricket, basketball, hockey, tennis, volleyball, table tennis, baseball, football and rugby, and golf.

The Ending

Whew! That was weird!
Okay, now you know all there is to know about sports.

Wait, Arlo! There's more!

WHAT?!

We put a lot of weird fast facts about sports in this book. But we didn't have room for *everything*. Kids can go to their school library or their public library to learn lots more.

 Go to the library? Are you out of your mind? Libraries are boring. Learning stuff is boring.

No, learning new things is cool, especially when you're learning about things you like. If you don't want to go to the library, all you have to do is go to a computer. Poke around. There's lots of cool information on the internet. All you have to do is search for it.

 Searching for stuff is boring. Why can't a truck full of computers fall on your head?

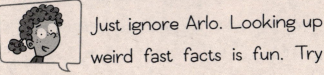 Just ignore Arlo. Looking up weird fast facts is fun. Try this: search for "weird facts about . . ." anything in the world. If you look up weird facts about elephants, for instance, lots of things will come up. Like this one: an elephant can swim twenty miles in a day—they use their trunks as natural snorkels!

 Your *face* is a natural snorkel.

The best part is that it's fun to impress grown-ups with how smart you are. If you take just about any fast fact in this book and tell it to your mom or dad, they probably won't know it. It will blow their minds! You see, grown-ups think kids are a bunch of dumbheads who don't know anything. But they're wrong!

So poke around and learn lots of new fast facts on your own. Maybe, if you work really hard at it, someday you'll know as many fast facts as Arlo and me.

But it won't be easy!